IN THE
NATIONAL INTEREST

General Sir John Monash once exhorted a graduating class to 'equip yourself for life, not solely for your own benefit but for the benefit of the whole community'. At the university established in his name, we repeat this statement to our own graduating classes, to acknowledge how important it is that common or public good flows from education.

Universities spread and build on the knowledge they acquire through scholarship in many ways, well beyond the transmission of this learning through education. It is a necessary part of a university's role to debate its findings, not only with other researchers and scholars, but also with the broader community in which it resides.

Publishing for the benefit of society is an important part of a university's commitment to free intellectual inquiry. A university provides civil space for such inquiry by its scholars, as well as for investigations by public intellectuals and expert practitioners.

This series, In the National Interest, embodies Monash University's mission to extend knowledge and encourage informed debate about matters of great significance to Australia's future.

Professor Margaret Gardner AC
President and Vice-Chancellor,
Monash University

WAYNE ERRINGTON & PETER VAN ONSELEN

WHO DARES LOSES: PARIAH POLICIES

MONASH UNIVERSITY PUBLISHING

Monash University Publishing
Matheson Library Annexe
40 Exhibition Walk
Monash University
Clayton, Victoria 3800, Australia
https://publishing.monash.edu

Monash University Publishing brings to the world publications which advance the best traditions of humane and enlightened thought.

ISBN: 9781922464637 (paperback)
ISBN: 9781922464644 (ebook)

Series: In the National Interest
Editor: Louise Adler
Project manager & copyeditor: Paul Smitz
Designer: Peter Long
Typesetter: Cannon Typesetting
Proofreader: Gillian Armitage
Printed in Australia by Ligare Book Printers

A catalogue record for this book is available from the National Library of Australia.

WHO DARES LOSES: PARIAH POLICIES

How do sensible policies that have worked well in other parts of the world become pariahs in Australia?

Each country has a political culture more accommodating to a particular policy mix, whether it's the overall size of government and the welfare state, or policy experimentation versus stability. While Australia's political class has a self-image of being reformist and fair, the current record is anything but. Australia has had world-leading policy successes that have been adopted elsewhere, such as tobacco labelling, and our response to the global COVID-19 pandemic has been among the best in the world. In other cases, however, substantial initiatives like the National Broadband Network and the National Disability Insurance Scheme (NDIS) have received the legislative nod but struggled at the implementation stage.

Politically, the outlook for policy reform looks precarious. Labor's failure to get a moderately ambitious policy agenda across the line at the May 2019 federal election threatened to usher in another era of policy timidity. Scott Morrison in many respects embodies the limitations of contemporary Australian politics: spin as a first instinct, little policy imagination, and a risk-averse approach even after a solid election win. Of course, there's much more to policy innovation than electoral politics. Only parts of the Hawke–Keating agenda of the 1980s was put to the electoral test. We shouldn't expect political leaders to show courage—to use a term currently in fashion—when the electorate and the media reward a more conservative approach. There is something to be said, though, for relying on the political advantages of incumbency and the extensive machinery of government to conjure the combination of policy ideas, political support and skill at implementation which is essential to sustained political change. This gives political leaders greater control of policy debate in a media environment that rewards short-termism. While hardly an example to inspire young political activists, the last Labor federal government did progress modest election proposals on broadband and disability insurance into substantial programs in government. On the other hand, when it came to carbon emissions trading, a bolder policy from the Opposition couldn't be sustained. Problems such as climate change and inequality will demand responses, though.

As well as discussing pariah policies that would raise more revenue in an efficient and equitable manner, this book considers the problems in our political system that can prevent good policy from being adopted. Some of the political limitations to policy boldness are well known—hyper-adversarialism, a political class obsessed with published opinion polls, and the related leadership instability. The major parties may have learned their lessons about leadership, particularly with the prime ministership having resembled a revolving door for a decade—not coincidentally, a decade of carnage that coincided with some execrable policy debate over the Budget and climate change, in particular. And the adversarial style over climate change can't be sustained. Nor, in light of the spending during the pandemic, can the mirage of a balanced Budget continue to be a policy end in itself. Along with the states, the federal government showed a good deal of policy flexibility when faced with the COVID-19 crisis. Perhaps Australia's policy muscles are in better shape after the vigorous exercise of 2020.

The policy proposals in this book have been battle-tested to a greater or lesser degree in comparable countries. Some, such as a universal basic income, are embryonic but are being discussed precisely because existing welfare policies are struggling in a globalised, high-technology economy. Many, such as taxes on carbon and sugar, have earned pariah status in Australia. For this to change, a reckoning of the type of country we want to be will be essential.

A UNIQUE OPPORTUNITY

The COVID-19 pandemic and its impact on state and Commonwealth budgets presents the Australian Government with a unique opportunity to deliver good public policy. Instead of fiddling around the edges of policy change, we have a once-in-a-generation chance to reset the way policy is made and delivered. The pandemic has provided an important reminder of what governments can do well—and of some of the things that only government can do.

The budgetary impact of the pandemic has swept aside a bipartisan myth about debt and deficit, as well as the role of the Reserve Bank. The pandemic may also have provided the catalyst for sensible tax policy. Too often, reforming ideas, especially in the theatre of tax reform, get met by criticism that they aren't revenue-neutral. That is, they will cost the Budget in the short term, which makes them politically unpalatable in an era of shallow, misinformed debate about needing to get budgets 'back in the black'. With a balanced Budget no longer just around the corner, as it was purported to have been since the Abbott government was elected in 2013, budgeting for the medium term will come back into fashion. In the wake of the extraordinary spending decisions made during 2020, the years ahead will have wall-to-wall deficits anyway, and our politicians have become resigned to that fact. So too has the public, who are no longer drawn into the political combat of tearing down one side of politics or the other for 'fiscal recklessness'. All of this is not an excuse for such recklessness. It's a prompt for a more sensible debate about the value of deficits and debt, revenue and spending, without the talisman of a budget surplus as the overwhelming goal.

If political debate doesn't hinge on the Budget, where should politicians and the public look for effective policy? While dozens of ministers get to stride the corridors of power and ride in the white car with the flag on the bonnet, most don't leave much of a mark. The same goes for the ministers who are quickly captured by their departments, no matter how many ideas they floated early in their political careers. Even the few who rise to become prime minister often don't really achieve a lot.

That is why real reforming governments and their achievements stand head and shoulders above the rest. While we think of individual leaders and their signature policies, much more goes into the achievement of policy change. Bob Hawke oversaw important microeconomic reforms and the Prices and Incomes Accord with the unions. Paul Keating was responsible for the introduction of superannuation. John Howard broadened the tax base with a goods and services tax and reformed gun laws. Kevin Rudd said sorry to Indigenous Australians. Julia Gillard introduced a price on carbon—only for Tony Abbott to repeal it; the NDIS is a more enduring legacy for Gillard. Malcolm Turnbull oversaw the introduction of same-sex marriage, although by the time he did so Australia was already a global laggard—and really it was the people's achievement anyway, via a popular plebiscite.

We have to go a little further back when surveying prime ministers to zero in on some of the most meaningful reforms that have shaped Australia, certainly in terms of social policy. Gough Whitlam introduced universal health care and free university education. The former continues today while the latter has been replaced by the Higher Education Contribution Scheme, but the purpose of ensuring accessibility has been maintained. The capture of the modern politician by bureaucrats has evolved, as politicians these days are less impressive and have narrower pre-parliamentary careers than they once did; the political advisers they surround themselves with are more callow and partisan; and government departments are larger and more controlling. Yet the standards of entry into the public service are lower than they once were. On the plus side, it is a more diverse workplace.

The media age we live in means that politicians are forced to spend more time acting as performing seals: fronting the cameras, practising their lines and immersing themselves in the theatre of politics. It's the art of the superficial, and it dramatically reduces the time spent thinking about bold policy reforms, which is to say nothing of the time MPs spend attending party events. Political fundraising, for one thing, has long been a blight on democracy, as ministers sell their time to the highest bidder. The political class denies that selling access buys influence, but that is at least the perception in the community, and it contributes to disillusionment with the body politic.

The very nature of the modern news cycle makes bold reform that much harder, with the instant unpicking of ideas on often tedious grounds, with claims and counterclaims that the numbers don't stack up. But the numbers won't stack up unless they've been put through rigorous departmental modelling, which often leaks, killing ideas in their infancy. This reality also reduces the chances of the Opposition developing meaningful policies, because they don't have access to such resources. Bill Shorten's 2019 defeat with a robust agenda makes it less likely that we'll see challengers be so bold in the future. This in turn means that governments become our only hope.

One good thing to come out of the global recession caused by the coronavirus is the chance to re-embrace meaningful reforms. This is the subject of renowned economist Ross Garnaut's new book *Reset: Restoring Australia after the Pandemic Recession*. Garnaut's prequel to *Reset* was his book *Superpower: Australia's Low-carbon Opportunity*, which was about the opportunities associated with pursuing economic reforms around climate change action—and the opportunity costs of not doing so. The new book is Garnaut's attempt to explain why we must now consider otherwise radical ideas that the political system usually renders impossible to achieve, including a universal basic income and replacing corporate tax with a tax on cash flows. Someone who has been writing about and implementing policy for as long as Garnaut knows that the best policy proposals can flounder because of base politics. As Bob Hawke's economics adviser, he served during a time of crisis in the domestic and international economy that actually encouraged a new policy direction—one in large measure not foreshadowed during Labor's 1983 election win—but which also meant that second-best policy solutions had to be swallowed. Subsequent opportunities for innovation, caused either by economic downturns or by the riches courtesy of the mining boom, produced relatively little.

We have already seen a lot of policy innovation as a result of the pandemic. Think about the tens of billions ploughed into JobKeeper and by contrast how difficult it can be to justify new initiatives worth a fraction of that amount. Yet the window of policy opportunity is by definition limited. While there was controversy about just how quickly JobKeeper should disappear, it was always designed to be temporary. Restarting the economy post-pandemic, though, provides politicians and policymakers with a chance to institute meaningful reforms that, while they might poke a further hole in the Budget in the short term, come with huge long-term benefits. Garnaut articulates the case for a universal basic income on just such a premise, as do we, making the point that yes, it is initially expensive, but over time the impact on the participation rate, innovation and entrepreneurial spirit pays huge budget dividends. Which is to say nothing of its value as a means of reducing inequality.

THE POLITICS OF POLICY

Decades of faltering policy efforts in Australia have left a backlog of ideas. For many countries, the global financial crisis was a catalyst for reform. In particular, the balance between the free movement of capital and the social equality required to sustain democracy has been the subject of many academic books. Australia has some great think tanks which adapt such ideas for the domestic environment. They also monitor public attitudes to tax, spending and government performance, and consider how policies implemented overseas might work in Australia. There is an ideological edge to think tanks that should be welcomed, rather than writing off their ideas as biased.

Since most prime ministers see themselves as potential reformers, there is also no shortage of reports from both government and independent sources. Often, though, these reports leave out the most important part of policymaking—the political process itself. Mastering the politics of policy is, of course, the job of political parties and it is here that Australia has been found wanting.

Take the Rudd government, for example, which with a solid majority was keen to embrace reform. Rudd commissioned then Treasury secretary Ken Henry to look into taxation options, released a Green Paper on carbon emissions reduction, and relied on Treasury to design a mining super profits tax. But in spite of the value of the Henry Report, it's a case study in how not to change public policy. That so little legislated policy resulted from all this activity was due to a combination of poor design—the mining tax was ridiculously complicated—poor communication skills, interminable government processes, and of course leadership tensions.

Coalition governments are less ambitious when it comes to reform, but Tony Abbott famously commissioned reports on tax and federalism which struggled to see the light of day. The Howard government congratulated itself on introducing a GST, which most other developed countries had done decades beforehand, but whose politics had proved too challenging in 1985 and 1993. However, once the broad-based consumption tax was in place, less attention was paid to the true reform, which was the replacement of less efficient charges mostly levied at the state level. After the introduction of the GST, the Commonwealth had the revenue but passed it on to the states without conditions.

Of course, policy reports don't disappear just because the politics of the day prove too difficult. Just as the Campbell Report into the financial system was waiting for the incoming Hawke government to implement many of its findings, the Henry Report remains an excellent discussion of Australia's taxation options.

WINNERS AREN'T REFORMERS

It's a necessary truism that being in politics is about winning government. Minor parties and independents might only work for their constituencies, either geographical or issues-based, but the majors aim to win government.

The Labor Party has lost seven of the last nine federal elections in Australia and is on track to make that eight out of ten, perhaps later in 2021. Such failure is an under-discussed phenomenon in modern Australian politics, especially in the context of the impact on the policy debate. In a two-party system, which is therefore a two-horse race, winning only 20 per cent of elections is simply woeful. In the modern era it has made Labor less ideological and less policy driven. In turn, the Coalition has seized on this failure, to the point where it has become more focused on winning than on reforming, playing to its strengths and Labor's weaknesses.

When you consider that one of the only two victories Labor has had during the past quarter-century was to form a minority government (the Gillard government in 2010), the scale of the problem is amplified. Labor has managed to form a majority government only once since its 1993 win under Paul Keating's leadership. That was Kevin Rudd's 2007 victory. Time and time again, Labor has come close to winning but doesn't quite get over the line.

Shorten's big-picture plans—limit negative gearing, dividend imputations and capital gains tax concessions—were successfully attacked by a small-target government. As a result, it's unlikely that any opposition party will pursue similarly bold ideas anytime soon, notwithstanding the fact that Shorten as an uncharismatic leader contributed to the defeat. The Morrison machine unpicked Labor's appeal with the mainstream and carved out a third term for a thoroughly unimpressive and divided Coalition government, one that now appears to be invincible electorally despite lacking any sort of vision for the future.

This is the problem with modern Australian politics. The progressive side of the two-party divide is too inept to apply adequate pressure to the conservative side, meaning conservatives stay in government without lifting their game. Poor opposition makes for poor government. The Westminster system needs a strong opposition to hold a government to account and keep it on its toes. Equally, when progressive governments don't get their professional act together, they make it easy for conservatives to fearmonger their way back into office without time on the opposition benches to reflect on party philosophy and intent beyond attaining power for power's sake.

Professionalisation has also had the perverse effect of attracting a less ideological, more careerist politician. This shift in pre-parliamentary personnel and terms of service has in turn reduced the willingness of elected MPs and senators to pursue transformational policy goals. They choose instead to be transactional representatives, extensions of the public service. It is much harder to build a career as a politician when taking unproven or radical ideas forward for consideration.

The changing nature of the media is also a problem in modern politics. It is more 'gotcha' driven, less mainstream, and so less willing to pull in behind big ideas, all at a time when voters have reform fatigue because of the extent of the changes that immediately predated the modern era. Those Australians lived through the tumult of the Whitlam years, the economic and social hubbub of the Hawke years, and the early tax and industrial relations moves of the Howard era. And because they locked in Australian prosperity and social opportunity, they breed complacency.

Which all means that as a nation, right at the very time we need bold ideas to manage our way out of a pandemic recession and its aftershocks, we are burdened by a timid Labor Opposition and a government more intent on winning than reforming.

Right now, Australia needs to be open to all manner of policy objectives, to come out of the other side of the pandemic well equipped for the brave new world that lies ahead. Convincing queasy voters that the medicine they really need is more reform, when they just want bed rest after such a difficult year, won't be easy, but that is the job of leaders. However, we have a Prime Minister who, when addressing the National Press Club in February 2021, told those in attendance that he had no plans to do things like increase taxes because that wasn't tax reform. He said the biggest thing he learned during the pandemic was to listen more, which appears to mean following the populist sentiment rather than providing leadership.

Morrison's characterisation of tax increases as not constituting tax reform showed a profound misunderstanding of how this actually works, which is alarming for a Prime Minister who is also a former treasurer. Of course it involves increasing taxes. That's what Howard did in 1998 when campaigning for a GST. The key is to use higher taxes in some areas to reduce less efficient or distorting taxes in other areas. It is to find new ways of taxing that ensure governments have enough revenue to do the things they need to do, and ditch outdated taxes that no longer serve the purpose they once did. That is a Liberal agenda, or at least it should be. Equally, Labor can fight against that agenda by making the case for enlarging the scope of government, if that's what it really believes. It can propose increasing the tax-to-GDP ratio by claiming that more is expected of modern governments, convincing citizens to accept that the taxes they pay must go up to safeguard the services they want. These are obvious elements of the social contract between governments and citizens.

Our policy ideas—from taxing the family home and inheritance, to commercialising the ABC, and simplifying the welfare system to the point of almost removing it altogether—aren't going to be presented in green or white paper form. That is the job of government, after the always laborious task of modelling options to figure out how to achieve policy ends. We simply seek to selectively challenge the conventional wisdom, which in some policy areas is presented with certainty domestically, even though there are myriad alternative ways of doing things being applied overseas. In an era when the role of the expert has been elevated by the COVID-19 pandemic, it is time for experts to assert themselves, and their ideas, in areas beyond health policy.

NEVER WASTE A CRISIS

In times of crisis, people are said to be more willing to accept change. And so the few remaining Liberal MPs with strong ideological views and values are increasingly demanding that the COVID-19 crisis not be wasted. That is, they want economic reforms to be vigorously pursued, even if doing so costs the government support at the ballot box. Their argument is that power for power's sake is meaningless, an ideological world view that butts up against the traditional conservative position that staying in office to keep Labor out of office is an end in and of itself. For while the Liberal Party of the 1980s and 1990s was dominated by ideologues, before and since that time, traditional conservatism has reigned supreme within the party room—especially when the values and views of the Nationals have been incorporated into Coalition decision-making.

With the nation's economy having been in recession in 2020, and unemployment and debt higher than before it, Australia can no longer be complacent about its status as the 'lucky country'. To be sure, we have been lucky, being better placed than most going into this COVID-induced downturn and geographically well positioned to pivot quickly enough to avoid the worst of the health implications of the virus. But as the world wrenches itself out of the downturn, we will see marked differences between nation-states regarding what levers they pull on the policy front.

If there is a theme binding our pariah proposals, it is Australia's fading sense of egalitarianism, always overstated yet undoubtedly part of the national ethos.

The concept that unites the Left and the Right behind specific policy proposals is equality of opportunity, because the idea that governments should seek equality of outcomes will not garner widespread support. Still, genuine equality of opportunity is an important step along the way, and also something which conservatives find it difficult to argue against. Indeed, rhetorically, it is essential to the support for a modern global economy. In some areas, particularly education, the pillars of equality of opportunity have been crumbling, and so our taxation proposals are geared towards restoring some sense of fairness.

On a similar note, opportunity and poverty reduction rely on high levels of demand and employment. Policies would rightly keep their pariah status if they were to provide disincentives to work and employ. The pandemic, while a bigger health risk for the elderly, has disproportionately financially hurt young Australians and women, two of the cohorts who would most benefit from a well-structured universal basic wage. According to budget forecasts, come 2025, Australians will have lived through the longest period of stagnant real wages in our history. Any policy that addresses that problem is surely worth a look, isn't it? In contrast to the problems young Australians and the marginalised face, those with established wealth have done very well out of long-term low interest rates, strong share market dividends and growing house prices.

Furthermore, reinvigorated trust in government encourages an active policy agenda with less pervasive political risk than that we have seen faced by successive governments since 2007. For some time now, surveys of public attitudes to government taxation and spending in Australia have shown that a majority believes in more spending on government services. However, middle income earners, based on their own experience of household budgets, don't feel as though they can contribute more. The key to this conundrum lies in a fairer system. There is a strong perception that the corporate sector and wealthy citizens don't pay their fair share. We see this when looking beyond the question of taxation to climate policy: someone else should pay. However, were the system perceived as fairer and the benefits of higher spending clearly identified, policy could move in the right direction. A good example of this was the increase in income tax earmarked for the NDIS. A potentially divisive debate was avoided because the hard policy work had been completed by the Gillard government. There was widespread consensus within state and federal governments, the third sector (organisations that belong to neither the public nor private sector), and members of the public directly affected that a new direction was needed.

Not all policy areas lend themselves to this sort of harmonious outcome, and the NDIS itself has hardly been a roaring success in the implementation phase. However, in terms of governments working towards consensus for a defined outcome—taking advantage of public trust in government to fill a need—it's hard to beat.

Climate change is the obvious area where revenue, spending and other government instruments have to come together to achieve policy outcomes in a way similar to the NDIS. And this is another way in which some proposals are pariahs, at least for public policy purists. Hypothecation, the elegant name given to earmarking revenue for specific spending purposes, is really a myth. There is no vault in the Treasury where the funds from the increase in the Medicare levy are kept for spending on the NDIS. Nor, for that matter, is the Medicare levy quarantined for health spending. However, given the way in which politics has been the element in the policymaking process that has most often cruelled promising ideas of late, getting public support for pariah policies needs this kind of myth-making. Earlier iterations of climate levies spent so much on compensation that the links between revenue and spending were difficult for the public to trace. A simple quid pro quo linking tax and spending might be more politically feasible. Most of our examples, though, are more defined. They contribute to a greater whole but could be adopted on their own as a contribution to a better policy approach.

There are certainly plenty of good policy ideas around, with lots of empirical evidence from overseas about what works and what doesn't, and possible solutions to the impasses that can give rise to a pariah. The system of government itself, though, needs to be able to design and implement policy.

While there is room for constitutional change, most notably with respect to Indigenous recognition, the COVID-19 pandemic has shown that Australia suffers primarily from a lack of political will. The system can be responsive in a crisis. As the crisis atmosphere of the pandemic recedes, though, government accountability will play a crucial role in ensuring that quality policy is on the public agenda. The National Cabinet will see states and the Commonwealth challenging each other for relevance. Independent agencies must keep the sense of urgency that has put pressure on governments over issues such as aged care and financial institutions.

One common observation about pandemic politics has been that the state governments have played just as important a role as the Commonwealth. Their premiers, health ministers and chief medical officers have proven essential. The problem with Australian federalism has been in its design. Powers are specified at some length for the Commonwealth, but few are detailed for the states. Combined with the Commonwealth raising the lion's share of taxation, this has created a mismatch between the states as direct service providers in health and education constrained by policy and funding dominated by the national sphere.

During the pandemic, these problems were largely avoided. The states were responsible for enforcing social distancing, while the Commonwealth was more active in resource-intensive policies such as JobKeeper. Failures in aged care, where some responsibilities are shared, was sheeted home to the feds. Quarantine was a more vexed policy area because it involved common responsibilities; or, more precisely, the states took up power in this area and there wasn't much the national government could do about it. Where the states don't need the Commonwealth's money, they can behave as sovereign entities, at least in a crisis atmosphere.

However, as things return to normal, long-standing problems with the division of power and revenue will return. States continually grizzle about a lack of resources, but when prime ministers suggest returning taxing powers to the states, the premiers tend to run for the hills. It may be time to bring this issue to a head. The National Cabinet might be the right forum for finding a solution to vertical fiscal imbalance, as part of a more general discussion about revenue levels and options. It's not as though national governments see their taxing powers as an unalloyed good. Prime ministers have long realised that greater balance in this area would help all concerned.

Once again, there are possibilities for both the Left and the Right. States can only find the optimum level of spending where they have the responsibility to find the revenue. If states want to spend more money, they will have to deal with the political consequences of raising it.

Policy ideas emerge both from within government and from independent sources. A review of existing policies, too, is something that can arise separate from government. It might come via formal reviews that the executive feels pressured to hold— independent inquiries or royal commissions—or through external bodies such as universities, or those with the relevant expertise providing assessments of policy performance. But while these can be useful exercises, they are often the product of governments avoiding accountability, delaying the inevitable, or simply solving short-term political problems with an inquiry. Other government review processes seem compromised—mates are brought in, or senior public servants who know what is expected of them provide the government with what they want. Regarding the wider public sector, the culture of spin is such that an honest assessment of policy performance can't come from within government departments.

One body whose value has been repeatedly underlined is the Australian National Audit Office, which supports the auditor-general. For its troubles, this organisation has had its funding cut. That a government can come under so little pressure for its thin-skinned response to adverse reports—from the ANAO or the ABC, for example—speaks to an essential problem with the quality control of public policy. The general public is indifferent to matters of process, and this is unlikely to change. It is up to the parliament to ensure that, while the executive needs to be free to take the lead in responding to policy challenges, ministers and departments are only one part of a complex chain of actors responsible for designing, implementing and reviewing policy.

Much has in fact been written about the capacity of governments—the public service and ministers in particular—to deal with the volume and complexity of policy challenges in the contemporary world. While there has been a hollowing out of the public sector in the name of smaller government and privatisation, there are enough success stories to build a case for optimism. On the other hand, can state capacity be blamed for policy failures such as the mining tax or climate change? Policy networks—the constellation of policy actors from the public, private and community sectors—have to an extent replaced the public service as the generator and testing ground for policy proposals; the Committee for Economic Development of Australia, for example, is at the centre of a longstanding economic policy network. Clearly, in some policy areas, these networks have failed the public interest. In fast-moving policy areas, it can be difficult for the public sector to keep up with the latest science and technology, which can leave governments relying on vested interests for advice. However, the balance of power when it comes to climate change, for example, can also change quickly, with new companies, think tanks, media outlets like Renew Economy, and universities adding to long-established interests like insurers to give voice to the growing scientific consensus and policy options. Governments should tap into these growing networks at the expense of those seeking to keep Australia in the climate Dark Ages.

The political institutions in greatest disrepair, however, are our major political parties. The party system is simply not fit for purpose in a complex modern world. The parties know this, so don't expect them to lead change when it comes to proportional representation in the electoral system, or to political donation laws and requirements for transparency. We return to these issues after presenting the pariah policies.

A UNIVERSAL BASIC INCOME

From Milton Friedman on the Right to Thomas Picketty on the Left, economists of all ideological shapes and sizes, across decades, have advocated for a universal basic income, or UBI—that is, a payment to all citizens, not means-tested and not contingent on one's employment status. Going as far back as the eighteenth-century writings of Thomas Paine, as well as advocacy by the likes of Bertrand Russell and Friedrich Hayek, the notion of a guaranteed minimum wage has received wide support. As Ross Garnaut recently wrote, 'the concept has no political colour'. It is undoubtedly, though, a pariah.

Australia is a good candidate for such a scheme. Some of our most intensive public debates have involved the interaction between the tax and welfare systems. Remember John Howard's 'barbeque stopper' in 2002? Howard's backbenchers heard directly from families who quickly lost child benefits when both spouses were working. Successive governments have only been able to deal with these issues, including childcare payments, when revenues were increased by making payments or the taxation tapering more generous. However, Australia's taxation system is prone to large swings in revenue. A more stable system, even if it's a more expensive one in the short term, is required.

The challenge has always been one of timing and priorities, and convincing the political class to consider such a radical policy change remains difficult. Shortly after John Howard was elected in 1996, a group of prominent economists wrote to the new prime minister pushing for a universal basic wage. But at the time, the political imperative was to pay down debt, with Howard having campaigned on that very theme. A UBI has therefore faced reasonable opposition in the past.

But if timing is everything, then now is surely the time for a universal basic wage to be properly assessed. With optimism about a diminishing pandemic and a leavening of the recession that it caused, the long and callow debate about debt and deficits in this country is being replaced by short-term disinterest in the issue. Blowing the Budget is the new black, but doing so for the purpose of introducing a UBI wouldn't be in vain. The considerable cost to the Budget in the short term wouldn't end up being money that disappears into the ether. The once all-important goal of revenue-neutral policy ideas is not a requirement in the current context, thereby giving us an opportunity to introduce groundbreaking reforms. Just as importantly, not all the costs of public policy are borne by the Budget.

The necessity to spend up big via programs like JobSeeker and JobKeeper has helped the public come to understand the value of short-term hits to the Budget, for an important purpose. That cultural awareness can therefore be developed to really shake up the way Australians both tax and spend. To be sure, historical advocacy for a UBI is not monosyllabic. There has been considerable disagreement about its design: How universal is universal? Should sections of society miss out? Should some of us receive more than others? What should the rate be? Will all other welfare payments be abolished? These variables will need to be properly considered. But the finer points of design are not a reason to junk the idea. They are a reason to debate it.

And the design, depending on which way policy-makers were to go, can mitigate some of the assumed higher costs of legislating a UBI. At first glance, fiscal conservatives only see the quantum of the spend: giving a set allowance to EVERYONE! But that seemingly fiscally reckless goal is watered down when we contemplate what it could replace: unemployment benefits, aged-care pensions, various other welfare allocations, and indeed the tax-free threshold workers currently get up to just shy of $20 000. If everyone gets a UBI, nobody needs to receive the tax-free threshold. But yes, it will still be expensive, at first in particular.

With wall-to-wall deficits in the budget out-years—those years beyond the budget year itself, and for which projections are made—now is the time to consider reforms that incur short-term costs for long-term advantage. The latter is why economists across the ideological spectrum have supported a UBI. To those, we can now add the likes of Amazon founder Jeff Bezos and Facebook's Mark Zuckerberg, who envisage a new generation of risk-takers being prepared to test their ideas when there is a floor past which they cannot fall if their business fails. Even the theoretical physicist Stephen Hawking advocated for the policy.

Just like the list of advocates, the arguments for a UBI are many and varied. As we pointed out earlier, the economic downturn precipitated by the COVID-19 pandemic has disproportionately hit the very cohorts in our community who would benefit the most from a UBI: the young, women, as well as people in part-time and casual work. One of the advantages of introducing this policy shift now is that it would inject more income into the economy at a time when consumer spending and business investment have been hit, providing a short-term stimulus.

The policy would increase labour force participation—although its opponents often assume the opposite. It also would provide an improved setting for adults to retrain and undertake further education. These outcomes should not be ignored, nor should the reality that the drive towards new technologies and automation may put traditional jobs in jeopardy. The gig economy means that job instability is more prevalent than it once was, all of which can be offset by a UBI that gives citizens social and economic stability. Increasing labour force participation at a time when it faces downward pressure should be a welcome potential outcome.

The World Bank has outlined five key advantages of a UBI. First, the removal of eligibility criteria avoids politically contentious decision-making about who qualifies for benefits and who doesn't. In doing so, errors are also removed, something that is particularly pertinent in Australia in the wake of the $1.2 billion settlement over the Robodebt fiasco, when Centrelink pursued debts that were found to be unlawful. Second, the stigma associated with unemployment benefits is removed when everyone receives a UBI. Third, transaction costs go down when selectivity of access is removed, thus creating more efficient processes. Fourth, there are labour force benefits to a UBI because, unlike payments which can be reduced as an individual increases their workforce participation, a UBI remains constant—it doesn't act as a disincentive to work. Finally, the World Bank points to a UBI as being less politically contentious than traditional welfare once instituted because everyone has access to it, thus avoiding the often grubby debates about 'bludgers' accessing welfare. Of course, this leaves unanswered the question of what the rate of any UBI should be, but that's politics in a democracy.

In a few short years, Australia will have lived through the longest period of real income stagnation in our history, and there is little evidence of that trend line shifting in coming years to avoid the unwanted record. This reality is the reason political pressure has grown for an increase in the minimum wage and the Newstart Allowance, but the introduction of a UBI is a better solution to wage stagflation. Lifting the minimum wage, while desirable for low-income earners, is hard in a country like Australia where the minimum wage is already high by global standards. The risk is that doing so puts some jobs at risk.

Australia's welfare system is complex, unnecessarily so. The requirements on the unemployed to qualify for benefits sees many applying for jobs they have little chance of securing, for the sole purpose of meeting the tests of payment eligibility. Aside from the physiological impact that process must have on the long-term unemployed, it bothers businesses too, forcing them to wade through applications which never should have been made in the first place. Some people on benefits spend more time focused on meeting eligibility criteria than on working towards genuine employment goals, or further education and training—they can spend as much time massaging a CV and accumulating job-search evidence as actually getting out there to find work. But if everyone received a basic income, this unnecessary process would be stripped from the system. The unemployed would therefore be free to pursue actual opportunities, or not. Those who currently fall between the cracks in the system, which often results in harrowing tales of subsistence living, would no longer do so—certainly not to the same extent. The political imperative to find savings in the welfare budget will apply no more.

A UBI also avoids the situation where someone who has recently lost a job might be denied access to unemployment benefits. It closes the gap between need and eligible access to the funds. It may even provide better incentives for younger Australians to participate in agricultural work, especially seasonal work, by not resulting in a loss of benefits because of temporary employment. And a UBI would encourage self-employment and entrepreneurial activities because those seeking to achieve such outcomes would at all times continue to receive the basic income. These are all good reasons to investigate the potential for implementation. So what might such a scheme look like in practice?

The reason why a UBI attracts support from across the political spectrum is that it deals with two different but related issues regarding the modern welfare state. One is the connection to citizenship—that the benefits from a capitalist society should be widely shared in order to maintain support, but this is also a right. The other is the way in which those principles turn into a bureaucratic mess as governments tinker, cut, expand and remove parts of the system depending on the perceived demands of the day. Good ideas on their own, or rational responses to policy problems, can make short-term sense but leave an overall set-up that is bewildering and unjust in its complexity. More bureaucrats end up being employed to interpret and implement the volumes of legislation and regulation that are inevitably designed to solve these problems, but they only add to complexity. In turn, the 'clients' of agencies like Centrelink feel as though they are any-thing but citizens with an entitlement to assistance. This is the state of affairs that led to the Robodebt scandal, which ended up not only being unjust but qualified as a false economy.

Finland completed a two-year experiment with a UBI in 2019. The results were mixed. Participants had improved health and social outcomes but were no more likely to be involved in the workforce. This would suggest that the world of work is more intri-cate than economic incentives might suggest, and any changes to welfare need to be complemented by education and workplace relations policies, as well as a greater emphasis from government on full employment. The results in Finland may also be a product of the shortness of the trial. Most economists acknowledge that real benefits to labour force participation, for example, will take time to manifest. The political difficulties in introducing such reforms were underlined when the Finnish Government refused an extension to the trial before the outcomes were even known.

The United Kingdom, meanwhile, has implemented one of the UBI principles in a benefit called Universal Credit. This is independent of work status and folds income support, child benefits and housing support into one application and payment system. It is strictly means-tested, though, and more varied in how it affects individual claimants. While the Right promotes Universal Credit as a streamlining of the welfare state and an incentive for work, the Left doesn't see it as a solution to poverty, so the all-important political consensus required for massive policy change isn't being achieved.

Naturally, once legislated, the most contentious aspect of a UBI would be the rate at which it should be set, as well perhaps as whether any citizens should be carved out of the system. Models proposed over the years have variously sought to exclude people on higher incomes or with higher levels of assets. This is usually justified on the grounds of trying to keep the cost of the system down. But exclusions also make achieving the policy reform harder. Few would disagree that the scheme should be limited to Australian citizens, or citizens and permanent residents. Equally, there is good reason to exclude citizens living abroad. And should people of different ages in different family situations receive variable payments? Logically, probably. But the more you tinker with the simplicity of the idea, the closer it gets to the complex welfare system it seeks to replace.

Advocates of an Australian basic income—language that is more familiar to the Australian ear than 'UBI'—have pitched a level of $18 500, considerably more than current unemployment benefits. High-income earners would lose the benefit—so this proposal wouldn't be universal. The emphasis is on reducing poverty, which runs into class envy as a political constraint. Such a system would cost about $125 billion net, which in a post-JobKeeper era isn't quite as eye-watering as it may have been in the past. That price tag over time would be mitigated by the benefits, both direct and indirect, that the UBI would create. Such a scheme would also bring Australia into the middle of the tax and spending pack of the Organisation for Economic Co-operation and Development—incidentally, the OECD has calculated that living above the poverty line in Australia requires an income of around $23 000, not $18 500. Given our propensity to enjoy spending at that level but to not want to pay the requisite tax, it's a challenge: a pariah. But it's not out of the question, as more and more problems with the current welfare system are exposed on a near-daily basis.

Just as the costs of the current system are more diffuse than those that appear in the Budget, the benefits of changing the system will also be widespread, though difficult to quantify. The symptoms of poverty in health, crime and violence also need to be accounted for. It is not just improved labour force participation and the encouragement of entrepreneurialism and retraining that matter. Reducing poverty has flow-on benefits which must be part of the moral arguments made about the welfare state.

More so than the costs, the UBI is a challenge for Australia's political culture. Past innovations in Australia's welfare state, often world-leading, were built around a foundation of work. The aged pension and the wage arbitration systems were based on the assumption that hard work should be rewarded. A two-party system featuring a party of labour and a party of capital buttressed this way of thinking. Social democratic parties featuring coalitions, including but not restricted to trade unions, in Europe and North America often took a different approach to welfare.

Julia Gillard as prime minister exemplified this ethos. She often spoke about the value of education and hard work, which meant that her policy concerning the work requirements for single mothers bothered even the most supportive feminists keen to talk up our first female prime minister. To the public, too, the idea of getting something for nothing is a hard sell. Welcome to the marketing challenges of politics.

Despite policy paralysis for many years, Australia has a rich history when it comes to reform—think giving women the vote, the unique nature of our electoral system, and universal health care. Equally, more than almost anywhere else in the world, Australians with established wealth have done very well out of recent low interest rates and escalating house prices. That said, with asset values rising the way they have in recent years, there has been a profound impact on inequality, a feature of modern economies most experts agree stifles growth and social harmony. The pandemic briefly hurt sections of this asset-rich class of Australians, but the rebound in the share market alongside a return to growth in house prices ultimately confirmed a divide that has long been widening.

Indeed, in overall terms, there is no hiding from the reality that Australia is a poorer country today than it was a decade ago, something that is true of many other countries. To avoid potentially leaving to our children a less-prosperous society than the one we inherited from our parents, the current generation of policy decision-makers needs to be bold. They need to be efficient regarding how production and distribution occur. A debate over a UBI falls well within that ambit.

TILL DEATH DO US PART

Louis XIV's finance minister, Jean-Baptiste Colbert, likened the art of taxation to plucking the maximum quantity of goose feathers with the least amount of hissing. Well, dead geese don't hiss. Or to use the language of economists, estate taxes are one of the more efficient of government imposts. What better time to pay tax than when it's too late to spend it on anything else? Yet this fairest and most efficient of taxes disappeared in Australia in the late 1970s after prize goose and then Queensland premier

Joh Bjelke-Petersen abolished that state's inheritance tax. Fearing a stampede of wrinklies moving up north for a tax-free death, all other states followed the Queensland precedent, and by 1981 Australia was death duty free.

Australia was alone in the industrialised world in doing without this most equitable of taxes, although not for long. Still, the estate tax, as the Americans call it, has survived the anti-tax onslaught there, though watered down with exemptions and threshold increases during three rounds of Republican Party–led tax reform, and an equivalent tax persists in the United Kingdom. Most industrialised countries have retained some sort of death duty, raising less than 2 per cent of total revenue. Such modest collections are disproportionately important because of the role they play in promoting equality and fairness in the system, which is vital to political support where there are related policy proposals that will adversely affect the middle class more directly.

The importance of inheritance taxes lies in how they help provide equity where rates of income and company tax have been repeatedly cut. Confidence in our system of government requires a strong sense that everyone is contributing. Death duties should form part of a tax and regulatory system that encourages productive investment over lazy family dynasties. Yet, in Australia at least, they have become a political weapon to be used against parties that aren't even planning for their introduction. This is therefore the ultimate pariah policy.

The disappearance of death duties here points to the limitations of Australian federalism. The states constantly complain about the lack of a secure tax base, yet they choose to forego revenue in the name of competitiveness, seeking to attract investment more likely than not to end up in Australia but not in any particular jurisdiction. States thus engage in auctions to attract and retain capital by reducing the few sources of revenue available to them. The rush to abandon death duties in the 1970s is a similar example. Partly as a result, states have become increasingly reliant on destructive taxes such as gambling royalties. A Commonwealth tax on estates would help reduce this needless competition for capital, provided there is agreement on how to distribute the revenue. Because of the historical evidence that our federation can lead to one state abolishing a tax such as death duties, thus causing a domino effect, it may be that like the GST, it is incumbent on the federal government to introduce a nationwide estate tax which it then distributes to the states.

States have limited sources of revenue, and most are regressive by nature. It has long been thus, ever since the transfer of income taxes to the Commonwealth during World War II. The Howard government was prepared to wear the political odium of pursuing a GST as an efficient replacement for indirect taxes and to reduce income taxes, passing the revenue on to the states. We need a similar magnanimity when it comes to death duties.

Such taxes were historically supported by classical liberals who favoured a modestly redistributive state. For colonial governments in the second half of the nineteenth century, death duties were a relatively easy tax to levy on a prosperous, fast-growing populace. Indeed, they were one of the first direct taxes widely imposed on Australians. World War I saw the introduction of the estate tax at the Commonwealth level, at rates varying from 1 to 15 per cent. Until the 1970s, the taxes enjoyed bipartisan support and therefore did not receive a lot of public debate. Liberals and social democrats agreed that the modest taxation of estates was consistent with a society interested in increased opportunity for all.

Yet the debate over death duties has a familiar ring to it, echoing many policy debates in developed countries in recent decades. As has happened time and again, the largest beneficiaries orchestrate a campaign to link their interests to those of the put-upon middle classes, reframing the debate into a tax on the death of the battlers. There is no Mark Latham around to label this 'aspiration', but the pattern of fear and loathing edging out rational policy debate is not new.

In the 1970s, the problems were blown out of proportion. High inflation undermined the exemptions for small estates, but these could have been easily changed or indexed. 'Double taxation' became the catchcry of opponents to death duties, never mind the wealth handed down over generations in a supposedly egalitarian society. Malcolm Fraser promised to abolish the Commonwealth tax during his successful re-election bid in 1977. In a sign of things to come, federal Liberal MPs championed small business and individualism in parliamentary debates, while the relationship between rugged individualism and inherited wealth was never fully explored. Neoliberalism, which was just clearing its throat when Australia ditched death duties, combined the classical liberal favouring of markets with political support for business large and small as a constituency. It remains a recipe for patchy policy outcomes.

Tax avoidance has come a long way since then, and designing an estate tax in a modern global economy has its challenges. With more wealth to inherit, there are more voters with an interest in estate planning. As the Henry Report pointed out, estate taxes may encourage consumption over savings. On the other hand, tax-free bequests are hardly an incentive for beneficiaries to work and save. Taxation would have a small but positive effect on the labour market.

Wealth taxes have been in vogue for some time now. At the 2019 US presidential primaries, Democrat candidates Bernie Sanders and Elizabeth Warren advocated for federal wealth taxes. More academics are now looking into their viability and ways to apply them better. Arguments for and against their application often come down to behavioural responses: the more powerful a behavioural response to a tax is, the more distortionary the effects can be. This is also an issue when it comes to sin taxes, as canvassed later in this book.

Wealth taxes in Switzerland provide an interesting analysis point, in terms of how they have impacted different regions based on their size and how vigorously the taxes have been enforced. A major problem has long been how easily they can be avoided. But because Swiss wealth taxes are so low—currently down to just 1 per cent—the need for avoidance is therefore also lowered. Beyond keeping rates low to discourage avoidance, enforcement mechanisms would be a key ingredient in their return in Australia. Potentially, the goal could be to impose the tax nationally, not state by state. This would avoid a repeat of the Queensland and then the national experience in the 1970s. As long as any federally imposed death duties were handed to the states, the tax policy outcome would also help address the problem of vertical fiscal imbalance in the federation. The global pandemic has reminded Australians that state power is important, but that hasn't changed the states' fiscal dependence on Canberra.

Since the abolition of death duties in Australia, the level of public trust in the political system—trust that is required to make significant policy changes—has declined. Bipartisanship or a sense of crisis seems essential. This is an obvious barrier to death duties being reintroduced, but it is not a good reason not to try. It simply means the politics are hard. In fact, the arguments for taxing estates have only become stronger as society has become wealthier and that wealth more concentrated. Longer life spans ensure that more wealth is consumed in retirement, but it also means that offspring are themselves older and more financially secure than when such taxes were first introduced. In addition, lower birth rates ensure that without policy change, ever-larger bequests will benefit smaller numbers of children.

Closing the loopholes around estate taxes ensures another round of complexity, by taxing gifts. The National Centre for Social and Economic Modelling has estimated that, as baby boomers continue to retire, bequests will double as a proportion of GDP to over $85 billion. Generous exemptions but no exclusion for the primary residence must exist. Of course, a legion of young people who see their parents' family home as the pathway to home ownership will bristle at this prospect. But we are all in this together, to quote the vacuous pandemic phrase, so the impact of the change will be broadly felt by the haves, with the have-nots no longer pushed further down the pathway to greater inequality. Bequest beneficiaries are wealthier and better educated than the population at large. The advantage they therefore receive from also inheriting a tax-free family home only exacerbates the inequality divide.

Economists debate the most efficient way to tax estates—in particular, whether the estate itself or beneficiaries should pay. Both options are fairly efficient. The most important political problem is the nature of the tax itself. However, we aren't finished with the need for reform once estate taxes are addressed.

TAXING THE FAMILY HOME

At the centre of one of Australia's most sacred myths is the family home. It represents security, continuity, and the ability of the Australian economy to provide a middle-class lifestyle to millions. To paraphrase Paul Keating, who was both a tax reformer as treasurer and a slayer of tax reform as prime minister, the parrot in the pet shop is talking about housing affordability.

The debate over housing affordability is hampered by two related issues, the first of which gets in the way of sensible discussion of any type of tax reform. The Liberal Party's sacred cow is that it is a party of low tax. But taxes have to pay for spending sooner or later. Unless governments are prepared to significantly and permanently lower their expenditure levels, taxes inevitably have to rise. The travails of the Abbott government in attempting to make expenditure cuts in some areas but actually increasing spending overall, is instructive. The point is that a broad tax base can't afford large, arbitrary carve-outs such as the family home. While many Australians see home ownership as the first step towards financial security, the benefits of the tax loopholes flow mostly to the wealthiest citizens.

The second policy constraint when it comes to the family home is that politicians have no intention of making housing affordable in the most straightforward sense—allowing prices to fall via any combination of supply- or demand-side measures. There is simply too much in the way of politics tied up in housing loopholes for governments to allow the redistribution of wealth that a sustained fall in housing prices might lead to.

The power of the property ownership myth is so strong that adjusting the tax treatment of investors as well as of owner-occupiers has proven difficult. Indeed, the Howard government made the affordability problem worse by halving capital gains taxes. And Labor's attempts at reform in these areas were met by a scare campaign at the last federal election. So where do we go from here?

Ideas on achieving fairer tax treatment of the family home have been wafting around for decades. They spring from think tanks, interest groups and government reports—and they are always ignored by governments. The notion of a tax on land being the most efficient way to go has long attracted support because it can improve both equity and efficiency. Moving from stamp duty on property transfers to a greater reliance on an annual tax on the unimproved value of land would swap one of the least-efficient government charges for one of most efficient. Labour could be more mobile in search of better wages and conditions, and a shorter commute; capital could be more lightly taxed. In an era of globalisation, one factor of production that isn't going anywhere is land. Tax on land is transparent, difficult to evade, and easy to calibrate for equity purposes.

As the Henry Report put it, land tax has the potential to provide cash-poor state governments with 'significant and sustainable revenue'. Revenue from stamp duty can be strong but it follows the cycle of the property market. It is an inefficient tax that stifles productivity. The extent to which states are reliant on this source of income is shown by the finding in the Henry Report that stamp duty on land transfers raised more than council rates and state land taxes combined. For states to have one of their largest sources of revenue subject to large variation plays havoc with their budgets. This is a major challenge when it comes to reforming this policy area under Australia's federation. However, older home owners could defer payment of the tax until after their estate was settled. This would be one way to help the theory of land taxes on the family home gel with the practical political challenges of such a policy objective.

The title 'stamp duty' betrays the antiquated nature of the charge. Stamp duty was for centuries widely levied on goods and services, but in Australia it is now largely restricted to the sale of property such as cars and homes. Why, then, are we stuck with a tax dating back to William of Orange's need for revenue to wage war against France in the seventeenth century?

Since The Greens backed the Abbott government's modest tightening of the assets test for the aged pension in 2015, the principal residence has remained exempt from the test. But as with land tax, there are numerous models that would allow the deferral of any liability without the need to sell the property immediately. These options should be even easier to embrace in a low interest rate environment. Pressure to realise the increased value of a house would be less problematic, of course, where stamp duty has been abolished, making any replacement property cheaper.

Changing from a poor to an efficient system will, of course, create winners and losers. And the sooner we accept that, the better. If politicians are not prepared to accept that some people will be worse off as a result of their policy reforms, they need to find another, less complex profession. Younger, more mobile professionals would benefit at the expense of retirees reluctant for a sea change or a tree change.

Reverse mortgages, for example, if priced right, could be a game changer, allowing people who really want to stay in their family home to do so and thus minimising the disadvantage. But let's be serious for a moment: retiring baby boomers who are well off enough to own their homes have lived through a period in which their wealth has exponentially soared because of the family home not being taxed. Low interest rates now hurt their retirement savings, but these could be used as a way of more easily accessing the cash locked into the family home—without the need to move or sell. If only a willingness to do so was embraced, or forced on them. One of the problems, however, is that the population bubble of baby boomers has a disproportionate impact on electoral politics.

When, early in 2015, then South Australian treasurer Tom Koutsantonis floated the possibility of stamp duty being replaced by a land tax, it only took a few days for him to be forced to rule out the measure. The Liberal Opposition and media swiftly found asset-rich but income-poor elderly folk who might be forced out of the homes bequeathed to them by family members, in spite of a review setting out possible compensation and deferral arrangements. Perhaps most damningly, *The Advertiser* accused Koutsantonis of a 'Joe Hockey moment', referring to the Commonwealth treasurer's abysmal sales job on taxes in the 2014 Budget. This episode was another example of how governments with an appetite for reform seek an honest appraisal of the available options through a review or a Green Paper, but after brashly declaring that nothing is out of bounds, they inevitably can't help ruling out unpopular options during what passes for policy debate in Australia.

Other jurisdictions have been bolder. The Australian Capital Territory and New South Wales have both addressed some of these issues. Canberra needs to attract labour from around the country to jobs in government and education. It also prides itself on its quality of life for families. The ACT Government has been plugging away at replacing inefficient taxes since 2012. Stamp duty on insurance has gone, and it's being phased out with respect to home purchases. The NSW move on housing stamp duty is more of a hedge but it may also be more politically appealing. Home buyers could choose between paying stamp duty up-front or as an annual levy, which would also rule out the double taxation that can occur with a shift in the tax mix.

While taxing the family home remains in the broader sense a pariah policy, in post-pandemic Australia it will at least increasingly be discussed.

It may be that, just as competitive federalism saw all the other states follow Queensland's abolition of death duties, the states will eventually be forced to provide a more rational tax treatment of land. We can only hope. With any luck, there won't be a repeat of the Rudd government's mishandling of the Henry Report's recommendation for a mining tax in 2010, which is the gold standard. After declaring, in his characteristic style, his desire for 'root and branch' reform, Rudd dithered over the Henry recommendation as an election approached. What should have been a popular charge on mostly foreign-owned corporations became the catalyst for Rudd's removal.

Governments that are skint lack the resources to conjure a more efficient tax system, while those that are flush lack the motivation. The last term of the Howard government saw billions wasted on income tax cuts and superannuation concessions. Granted, the hysterical reaction to its introduction of a GST would have tempered any politician's appetite for reform. Yet the GST example shows that reform is possible when governments have the resources and the political will. People do forget, however, what it took for that reform to make it onto the political agenda, and that the Howard-era reforms almost ended before they'd even really started. The landslide win the Coalition enjoyed in March 1996 was all but entirely taken away two and a half years later courtesy of the fight for GST reform.

The lesson many politicians of the future learnt watching what happened to Howard was: 'Don't reform if you want to retain a healthy majority'. This butted up against Howard's personal view that the GST fight saved his government, which otherwise was drifting aimlessly. But the more capable political observers of Howard realised that if you do want to embark on major reform, it has to come early in the life cycle of a government—they saw that with Howard, and with Hawke before that. Indeed, Howard's failure to entrench his late-term WorkChoices changes proved to this political grouping that late-term reforms aren't something long-term governments can achieve. WorkChoices was more complicated than that, but it's best not to burden these political thinkers with facts.

When we look at the Morrison government—a third Liberal PM leading a third-term Coalition government—it isn't hard to understand, in that context, why it's disinclined to embrace major policy reform. And despite the government already being long in the tooth, the Labor Opposition, badly burnt by its attempt to campaign for major reform at the last election, also isn't up for big policy changes. At least the idea of taxing the family home is one of the few areas in which states can pursue reform. Doing so would be easier with federal help, but we'll take what we can get.

THE CLIMATE EMERGENCY

'Once more unto the breach, dear friends, once more,' said William Shakespeare's Henry V, words that contemporary Australian political leaders can relate to very well indeed. The fraught politics of climate change has contributed to the downfall of every prime minister since John Howard, except one—Scott Morrison has avoided the curse, mostly by doing very little about the issue since becoming prime minister in 2018. Morrison is moving more slowly than a melting glacier, although at the time of writing, he did finally seem to be feeling the heat on climate policy.

The reason political leaders keep reaching for this third rail of Australian politics is that public backing of action on climate change has been strong and consistent. According to a recent Lowy Institute Poll, support for the proposition that climate action is urgently needed, 'even if this involves significant costs', has returned to levels last seen under Rudd. This option was for a time eclipsed by the idea that the costs should be minimised, but taking action regardless of the cost now has double the support of the more cautious formulation. Meanwhile, scepticism putters along at between 10 and 20 per cent, receiving much more than its fair share of media airtime.

What this polling shows is that Australians are responsive to leadership on this issue. Just as importantly, though, implicit in the public opposition regarding cost is the expectation that someone else should wear the cost—the ideal tax on carbon is one that consumers and corporations avoid paying. What might brave leadership look like given the extensive track record of the political risks involved in climate policy? As well as courage, there's another missing but essential link in Australian politics: transparency. Any new idea to price carbon and tackle climate change needs to be transparent. Anything less off the back of the past two decades won't fly.

One of the great counterfactuals of Australian politics is what would have happened if Kevin Rudd had met the Senate's failure to pass his Carbon Pollution Reduction Scheme with a double-dissolution election; or indeed, what would have happened had The Greens agreed to it, leaving the Opposition to fight its own internal war without the opportunity to block the legislation. Despite his 2007 win, which made him only the third Labor leader to take the party back into government since World War II, Rudd was a relative political novice. He had entered parliament less than a decade prior to his victory, had never held a ministerial role, and had been the Labor leader for less than twelve months before the election, so when the going got tough in his first term, Rudd panicked. He didn't think he would lose a double-dissolution election against Tony Abbott, but he was worried that he might not win by a big-enough margin. He was being advised by Labor's central office that other policy issues, such as the growing wave of refugees arriving by boat, were tightening the political race.

The problem for Rudd was that his timidity became a self-fulfilling prophecy. Voters believed his passionate plea that climate change was the 'greatest moral challenge of our time', which is why they couldn't understand why he was prepared to baulk at fighting an election on the issue. When Labor then watered down its policy on the matter, Rudd's personal numbers nosedived. It was the beginning of the end, one way or the other. The fact that Rudd didn't call an early election was a measure of how little he knew about the moves within his own party to relieve him of the burdens of office. Since gaining the leadership, he had had to take on the factions and the unions, despite achieving the repeal of WorkChoices. In short, Rudd wasn't loved internally even though the polls initially suggested the opposite in the wider electorate.

The CPRS proposal consisted of eleven separate bills, which was just too complicated. When Tony Abbott assumed the Liberal Party leadership in late 2009, in no small part because of the way Malcolm Turnbull had negotiated with the government on climate change, the legislation was doomed. Rudd had his double-dissolution trigger, but instead of using it, he reintroduced the bills in early 2010 with further exemptions for fuel. Even this pale imitation of urgent action was then delayed by the prime minister. Buried in the Treasury analysis was the finding that the CPRS, after the compensation to industry, would have been a net revenue loser. Instead, the Coalition took into government in 2013 vague promises of 'direct action'. This would, in the style of the current government, involve picking winners and granting favours to well-connected industries. It was Abbott's cobbled-together alternative to Julia Gillard's carbon tax which transitioned into an emissions-trading scheme along the lines Rudd had first mooted.

The Greens were always concerned that the CPRS promised emissions reductions decades down the track, which was too slow for a party of the radical Left. One of those decades has now passed, with little action having been taken. However, those years have seen great improvements in renewable energy technology. The principle behind the CPRS—providing incentives for a reduction in emissions across the economy—is still necessary for significant cuts in greenhouse gases. The trends, be they in the science, international pressure, technology or the economy, are all welcoming of decisive action on Australia's part.

The CPRS was filled with concessions to big polluters to get them inside the system. While the Australian polity has remained resistant to a grand bargain on climate change, many of the underlying pressures have changed considerably since 2013, when Abbott triumphed over the renewed Rudd leadership. Yes, the coal industry has played a disproportionate role in climate policy over the last decade, and the urgency of that commitment may remain. But the coal industry now competes with well-heeled lobbyists from renewable energy companies and a host of industries from insurance to mining that can more clearly see the costs of a lack of action. BHP, for example, promotes its copper mining as an essential means to provide rooftop solar panels, notwithstanding copper's small share in the company's profits. Energy companies invest in wind and solar at levels undreamed of even under the projections of emissions trading. Export industries, which have been lining up for compensation under previous approaches, are now alarmed at the prospect of tariffs on carbon-intensive imports under the Paris Agreement.

Gillard's *Clean Energy Act* was a step in the right direction—it was simpler than the CPRS but still had a lot of moving parts. And such progress towards a carbon price was a condition of The Greens supporting Gillard's minority government. However, with the Opposition promising to repeal the legislation, companies were reluctant to invest. The cap-and-trade element of the scheme was never implemented, and tellingly, investment in coal continued throughout all of these policy perambulations. However, in spite of all this policy uncertainty, carbon emissions fell while the Act was in place. And now, around the world, sometimes in concert with sophisticated policy and sometimes not, investment in fossil fuels is being superseded by investment in clean energy.

In short, however much climate sceptics might deny the undeniable, there is overwhelming evidence that the drive towards more renewable energy and alternative fuels is gaining pace—more so than even the supposed climate change zealots predicted. In the 2000s, polluting industries could reasonably claim that decades of investment were at risk and compensation was warranted. Today, any industry that has ploughed investment into carbon-intensive production has done so at enormous commercial risk. It's no longer up to taxpayers to subsidise that risk. The moment is ripe for a reversal of the politics of climate change. So what needs to happen next?

We need to turn the CPRS on its head. Instead of trying to cover the whole economy, we must draw up a narrow list of inclusions to tax. Abbott reportedly pointed out the relative simplicity of a carbon tax compared with what Rudd was offering (and the emissions trading scheme that John Howard had taken to the 2007 election). Instead of pricing carbon to drive investment and beef up the existing schemes, a simple tax appealed to Abbott—before a simple tearing down of Gillard's broken promise to do just that became his raison d'être.

Both Howard's ETS and Rudd's jumble of letters came at a time when faith in the markets to solve the world's problems was much greater. What we propose is a continuation of the current interventionist approach, supercharged by a temporary source of revenue. Importantly, the legislation would need to have built into it clear provisions for when it becomes redundant. Take the first stage of the Gillard government's carbon price, essentially a tax on the fifteen or so largest carbon emitters. Politically, stress the concentrated and temporary nature of the scheme. Use the funds to subsidise clean energy investment. Hypothecation of petrol taxes has proven popular at the state level when accompanied by a time-limited commitment. Show exactly where the money will go. Learn from the mistakes made by myriad small grants programs by setting clear principles for the distribution of resources. Minimise the costs to rural areas but include them in the spending side of the scheme to demonstrate the viability of alternative measures.

Planning for the long term needs to happen alongside the temporary measures to ensure the comprehensive decarbonisation of key sectors. The Victorian and South Australian governments did just that in late 2020 by experimenting with charges on electric vehicles. These announcements were met with predictable squeals from green zealots and renewable energy lobbyists who would accept nothing but the unalloyed promotion of electric vehicles. It would be dishonest, though, to incentivise electric vehicles now and slug the owners later. Buyers can only beware if they have all the facts. Similar planning needs to accompany decarbonisation across the transport and building sectors, with incentives provided by the revenue stream gained from taxing carbon-intensive industries.

IT'S NOT AS EASY AS ABC

Public policy can't improve without a public sphere to facilitate quality debate. While the internet has provided limitless opportunities for those keen to engage in politics, it has also brought serious downsides. The mass media model was able to subsidise journalism through more lucrative commercial activities. The 'rivers of gold' classified ads and banner product placements generated revenue in ways media owners today can only dream of. But the internet has forced the disaggregation of much of this activity, leading to journalists being sacked in a decade-long bloodbath. The urgency of this problem means that government policy in this sector needs to concentrate on quality debate and investigative journalism. Public subsidy needs to reach beyond the current public broadcasters—like SBS, the ABC will have to generate more of its own revenue.

Our technological cornucopia gives enormous agency to consumers. On the one hand, policy specialists can discover new ideas and communicate with each other. The internet-facilitated public sphere, though, can divorce this rich discussion from the general public. This can be caused by narrow spheres being divided into specialised interests without the capacity to communicate effectively with citizens, or conversations taking place within Left- or Right-dominated subcultures. A bigger problem, though, especially in a compulsory voting jurisdiction like Australia, is that voters can be completely cut off from serious news. This provides the short-term risk of a poorly informed public, and the longer-term risk of a public sphere incapable of knowing what information is reliable and what is not.

We don't need to romanticise the mass media era when most people watched, read or listened to news on a daily basis to recognise that some form of public engagement is essential if a democracy is to serve its purpose. A vigorous public realm needs to expose vested interests, whereas mass media has a habit of becoming one of those interests. Many celebrated the loss of power of the 'gatekeepers' who make decisions about news values and priorities. But is the alternative really any better?

While social media allows many voices to be heard, those voices are thinly spread and are rarely able to replicate quality journalism—facts get lost.

Social media allows for the bypassing of gatekeepers, the greater dissemination of news media, and the chance for citizen journalists and alternative media to expand their reach. It is not, however, a panacea for a media industry under pressure. Social media provides opportunities for policymakers to avoid scrutiny by communicating directly with followers. But again, this is not a substitute for the decline of the mainstream media. Rather, it is an independent benefit that social media offers, albeit it can come at the expense of scrutiny. Donald Trump put a name to an age-old problem when he popularised the idea of 'fake news'.

To combat the rise of disinformation, quality journalism will have to be subsidised. But by who?

The Commonwealth made a start by requiring good-faith negotiations between big tech companies and local news producers, but as we discovered when Facebook closed down its Australia-based news feeds in February 2021, there is no single definition of news. Larger jurisdictions will at some point require the actual or de-facto break-up of information behemoths such as Google or Facebook, whether purely in terms of their commercial dominance or because of the unique importance of information in a democracy. In the meantime, governments need to again be proactive in shaping the public sphere in a way not dissimilar to the establishment of public broadcasting in the first half of the twentieth century.

The ABC's charter requires a comprehensive broadcasting service. In a highly specialised media environment, comprehensiveness may still be a virtue. It is also increasingly becoming highly contested. Public broadcasters will always debate the margins of what fashions they need to follow when it comes to entertainment, particularly with the nation becoming more diverse and culturally polarised. Similarly, there is little debate about whether news is at the heart of the public mission. Is it realistic, though, for a broadcaster that is being robbed of audience share by technology, to receive a growing share of the national pie? We agree that the public broadcasters have been underfunded for decades. However, there are more important demands on the public purse than for this problem to be solved simply by a reversal of the funding trend.

When it comes to news, the ABC has become more important in regional areas in particular. However, while the ABC News brand is vital as a marker of quality among the mass communication din, it can't be expected to carry the flag alone. Policy needs to encourage the production and dissemination of quality journalism across the nation, across platforms and technologies, and in a way that is inclusive of all demographics. But how?

Ironically, news seems to be everywhere. Between the ABC's own TV and radio news channels, Sky News, and commercial television's current fashion for endless afternoon news bulletins, there appear to be more outlets than ever. Social media amplifies this reach. Look closer, though, and the news is just being spread thinner than ever. State and regional news has become much more scarce, as have specialist reporters in areas like health and foreign affairs, whose knowledge is essential for holding governments to account in specific policy areas.

It has been a long time since commercial broadcasters funded sustained investigative journalism. Not since the rivers of gold dried up has this been financially supported to a point most news veterans would deem remotely adequate or broad-ranging enough. Even the better investigative journalism Australians can still enjoy isn't what it once was. With resources stretched, journalists chasing long-form stories can't afford to do their research and pull up short. There always has to be a story, which becomes a case of the tail wagging the dog. Gone are the days of a weeks-long or even months-long investigation that ultimately finds no wrongdoing. Now, even if it's not there, what can't be found, or manufactured, will be zeroed in on, amplified or sensationalised.

It's difficult to argue that a greater proportion of national funds should go to public broadcasters to produce entertainment in large supply elsewhere. ABC forays into such an approach have been rightly pilloried. But it's important to consider why the Coalition government has not paid a political price for starving the ABC and for engaging in endless culture war skirmishes over its content. As SBS has shown, subsidising public broadcasters with advertising while sustaining quality is possible. This is consistent with the principle that revenue-raising needs to be broad but not deep. As long as the commercial arm of any public broadcaster is kept away from the editorial decision-making, the two worlds can coexist in separate silos.

As a state-owned entity not subject to commercial pressures like its competitors—during a very difficult time for the media, incidentally—the ABC has become a media version of Thomas Hobbes' *Leviathan*. Yes, even as its funding gets crimped. A way around that involves copying the SBS dive into airing commercials. Advertisers would love to tap into the substantial ABC audience, and if done correctly, the criticism that ads would lower the tone of the ABC's present crop of investigative news services and high-end commentary programs would be revealed as nonsense. Many of these programs rate very well already, operating in a quasi-commercial way with eyes fixed on ratings, not to mention the fact that some of the ABC's best talent hosts and works on such programs. Alternatively, SBS and the ABC could be merged into a single broadcaster, thereby treating the services that SBS currently provides as an arm of the ABC on its multichannel services. This would substantially reduce duplication, freeing up funds for further investigations and usage of monies for public interest journalism. As long as the ABC charter was expanded to encapsulate the SBS offerings, little if anything would be lost to viewers and listeners. Rather, the reach of SBS programming that is retained would be expanded, and the commercial offerings to advertising would become even more attractive. There is a strong argument that were the ABC to compete on a level playing field with other commercial networks, those networks would have a market incentive to lift their standard of news coverage, in a bid to steal ABC viewers and their lucrative advertisers.

We can't expect the public broadcasters to monopolise public interest journalism. While the

ABC has substantial reach, quality journalism needs to permeate every nook of the internet to combat the falsehoods and spin which seem to be growing exponentially. A mechanism for supporting the production of news in outlets like *The Guardian* could help ensure that the truth has a fighting chance. Unfortunately, a good deal of fake news comes via the substantial resources devoted to government public relations and media advisers—often former journalists—across all political parties. The Commonwealth does have an existing set of Public Interest News Gathering grants amounting to $50 million, and a similar fund to support regional news—an area where the changing economics of the industry have had devastating effects, with public broadcasting doing little to fill the gaps in regional content. Tax deductibility that encourages philanthropic organisations to invest in journalism could also play a role; the Public Interest Journalism Initiative, itself a product of philanthropy, is producing useful proposals. As we have suggested in other policy areas, widespread small initiatives will need to accompany the big reforms to gain public support.

Without an active public sphere, public policy has no chance of improving. Public broadcasters play a vital role here, but a more robust set of institutions must be developed to ensure a well-informed citizenry and improved political debate.

THE SWEETEST TAX OF ALL

Sin taxes are nothing new. Designed to penalise bad behaviour, in theory they should discourage the use of products deemed harmful to individuals or to society in general. So it's no surprise that the World Health Organization supports the taxing of sugary drinks to help tackle obesity and diabetes. Opponents on the Left point to this proposal's regressive nature, to how such taxes penalise the poor without necessarily adjusting behaviour. Critics on the Right point to such a move as an example of the nanny state taking over.

But we already have similar sin taxes on everything from gambling to smoking to alcohol, and we don't see any moves afoot to reduce such taxes. In fact, it's a regular occurrence come budget time to see these taxes go up and up. The Left then loses its concerns about their regressive nature just as the Right forgets about the nanny state implications. In the case of gambling, the tax is built on an industry that could be banned. Not so for the other vices, with prohibition having taught us that doing so would simply move the practices underground and reduce the overall tax take of government. It is the poorest who can make the greatest health gains from this policy. This logic is why currently there is a push to legalise vaping, a harm-minimisation strategy that is taxable and would undercut any underground trading.

So why are sugar taxes not a live policy option? Simply put, it's because of concerns about the pressure that might be applied from powerful food industries. Indeed, in a bid to stave off the prospect of a sugar tax ever becoming a reality, the soft-drink industry has started moving away from its more sugary products towards low-calorie, low-sugar alternatives. It's a chicken-or-the-egg argument to work out what came first: the moral imperative of the shift, or the shift as a response to declining sales. We cynically suggest the latter.

On their part, governments have sought to substitute better labelling and industry disclosure for consideration of a sugar tax, but we wonder why they choose to go down that path. Doing so imposes cost burdens on the sector and, let's face it, most people don't read food product labels at the best of times. Refusing to institute a sugar tax is denying a clear-cut revenue stream advocated by experts such as the Australian Medical Association. The aim, as with other sin taxes, would be to reduce consumption and therefore future revenue—after a sugar hit to tax revenue—while eventually reducing spending on the associated health problems. And unlike addictive products like alcohol and tobacco, there are simple substitutes for sugary drinks in the form of artificial sweeteners. A sugar tax need not be pegged at the exorbitant rate of that on tobacco products to be effective.

The rise in obesity has become a global problem, especially in wealthy countries, and Australia is not exempt. In fact, among the OECD countries, we are one of the more obese nations, perhaps surprising given our sporting culture. The downsides to obesity are obvious: to one's lifestyle, mental state, and of course health. Given that Australia enjoys a universal healthcare system, the state—as much as, if not more than, the individual—is bearing the financial burden of what some experts now describe as an obesity epidemic.

James Muecke, the 2020 Australian of the Year, used his time in that office to raise awareness about the damaging impact of a high-sugar diet. It is ironic that during the first year of the COVID-19 pandemic, which had us listening to health experts more than ever, the Australian of the Year, himself a health expert, could barely attain 10 per cent of the platform previous awardees had received.

Taxes on sugary drinks have been adopted in dozens of overseas jurisdictions. A study of the 10 per cent tax in Mexico found a nearly 8 per cent reduction in consumption. The acuteness of their obesity problems saw a number of Pacific island states pioneer the use of sugar taxes. The United Kingdom has two tiers of sugar intensity that attract an increasing tax impost. The position of fruit juices in all this is politically vexing, since taxing those would upset multiple rural lobbies, not just that of sugar. But exclude fruit juices from the tax and beverage companies, according to evidence from India, will exploit the loophole. As we have stressed throughout, don't let the perfect be the enemy of the good.

Responding to calls for such a tax when he was prime minister, Malcolm Turnbull suggested that there were enough taxes on consumption already and policy needed to concentrate on education and awareness—in other words, collect revenue from somewhere else so as to spend money to deal with a problem that, as has been shown in other countries, can be addressed with a financial push. We do need to be mindful of the burden on Indigenous communities. Diet and obesity are hugely complex issues. Taxing sugar, on the other hand, is simple: tax sugary drinks at a relatively low rate and we consume less of them.

Seeing the writing on the wall, the Australian Beverages Council has announced plans for voluntary reductions over time. Let's help them along with a financial incentive that will have broad social benefits and contribute to the national bottom line.

WHERE TO FROM HERE?

The blame for the state of modern politics lies not just with the politicians but with journalists, commentators and voters as well. The selfishness of voters is only matched by politicians' grab for power, and journalists, while not entirely to blame for the way they cover politics, do share responsibility for the lack of focus on policy. In our view, there are three relatively simple ways to improve the situation, actions that will return politics to the art of governing with a policy focus: the tighter regulation of political parties; recognition that Australia has outgrown the two-party system and must reform its institutions to remake that system; and the need to institutionalise consultation within the law-making process. We have written about this before in an article for the *Griffith Review*, five years ago in fact. It is remarkable how little has changed.

To the extent that they turn their attention to it, Australians are not happy with how politicians go about their daily business. That's because the modern politician has expert knowledge about communicating, campaigning and focus groups, but little time or respect for one of the best traditions of government: the patient development of policy formulated with the assistance of a professional public service. Presenting as a small target to the electorate means that concepts like platforms and mandates have almost dropped out of the vocabulary of politics. As we discussed, Bill Shorten's failure to win the 2019 election with a larger-than-usual target will only exacerbate this problem. Where the notion of a mandate does surface, it's used as a simplistic device to help a government get its way in the parliament— to put pressure on the Senate to pass a government's proposed bills, ignoring the check-and-balance role the second chamber was designed to provide. Given how little detail there is about policies during election campaigns, it is doubtful that winning elections even equates to popular policy mandates in the first place.

The permanent campaign is a concept that the American political scientists Norman Ornstein and Thomas Mann first wrote about twenty years ago.

It involves the professionalisation of politics to a point where the participants become involved in a permanent election campaign—they use the media and the routines of politics to achieve the direct goal of re-election, throughout an entire electoral term. As a result of this professionalisation, there is a loss of pre-parliamentary career diversity in representatives, which narrows the intellectual outlook of the body politic and in turn has removed the ideological drive of modern politics. This results in limited representative choices for voters. In Australia, the major parties are dominated by careerists for whom election is the goal rather than the means of achieving one's goals. Retaining power has become more important than using incumbency to achieve goals. This has many impacts—on leadership theory, public policy and political stability.

Where once Liberals would accuse Labor of ideological and professional narrowness because of the large number of former union officials in the latter's ranks, now both sides are heavily laden with ex-staffers. And research on the pre-parliamentary careers of our politicians reveals that this is narrowing. The Liberal Party rarely preselects small business owners, partly because of more rigid factional groupings and partly because those small business owners have stepped back from political engagement. Both major parties are becoming less reflective of the constituencies they claim to represent.

To the extent that we read about diversity in the backgrounds of MPs in their parliamentary biographies, such career markers are more spin than reality, there for appearances rather than life experience gained. Too many MPs with backgrounds in larger organisations have worked within the media or government affairs divisions, rather than at the heart of business, learning the ropes when it comes to managing more than marketing.

On the Labor side, while ex-union officials continue to dominate parliamentary ranks, alongside ex-staffers, they are career union officials rather than those who have moved from the factory floor into official roles and then into parliament. This used to be a celebrated feature of Labor MPs. The working-class diversity that once made up for the narrowness of union domination within Labor's ranks is no more. Isolated exceptions help prove the rule.

The most concerning aspect of the professionalisation of politics is the disconnect we now see between politicians and the wider electorate, including those who vote for them. Our leaders know too much about politics and not enough about life.

The erosion of stability caused by professionalisation isn't only the fault of politicians. Because public comments by political leaders are increasingly scripted (and predictable), journalists covering such appearances often compete to seek out the real thinking behind the preprepared lines. They celebrate the 'gaffes', which American journalist Michael Kinsley defined as an accidental utterance of the truth, produced by politicians because they puncture the images that leaders and their advisers seek to project. Even politicians resent this charade. Not long ago, political scientists wondered whether this 'PR state' gave undue advantages to incumbent governments.

Enough complaining. Let's turn our attention to what to do about the problems identified. We are not seeking to revolutionise the system, but if politicians are unwilling to break free from the limits that professionalisation imposes, there are at least some parts of the system that can be improved to restore faith in politics amongst voters. Other Westminster systems have been much more innovative than Australia in reform and adaptation in modern times, which is a shame because Australia was once known for its innovation around voting and electoral systems. Australia is almost unique in lacking a bill of rights, for example; New Zealand and the United Kingdom have remade their respective systems in quite different ways. Constitutional change is notoriously difficult here. None of our suggestions necessarily require constitutional change, although such entrenchment could be useful. We offer three principles that would make the system more democratic and fairer and focus political parties on their underlying purpose of improving the lives of their constituents instead of occupying office.

Political fundraising has very little oversight, and it has numerous loopholes for parties to hide donors from the register, despite recent reforms. The conflation of party political roles and their duty to the state sees ministers using their power to raise funds for private organisations—the political parties they represent. Money buys access to these decision-makers, and while it might not buy outcomes, the perception that it does, or the potential that it might, should lead to effective reforms.

Buying time with a minister at roundtable discussions at state and federal party conferences is akin to the prostitution of our democracy, and the players themselves don't like it either. We even see lunches and dinners with political leaders sold off to the highest bidder at party events. Ministers are already under intense time pressure to attend such

WAYNE ERRINGTON & PETER VAN ONSELEN

events, engage with the media, position themselves with colleagues and perhaps even get across policy details—the last thing they want is to be rolled out as the bait at expensive fundraisers. But party officials who run election campaigns, and who have no accountability in political institutional frameworks, demand that ministers attend these events, and they have the authority to insist on it.

We need to acknowledge that the major parties that benefit from the electoral system aren't likely to change it, but change can and does happen. New Zealanders were deeply unhappy with their much more centralised set-up, and they were offered a choice of electoral systems. The complexities of the multi-member electorate, which better balances local representation with proportional representation, didn't frighten voters away from electoral reform. Education and genuine intent to promote change are key here.

While the dominance of the two-party system itself restricts input into the policymaking processes of government to select parties, the decision-making processes are even narrower. Policymaking hasn't just been restricted to the executive arm of government but has been narrowly cast within the Prime Minister's Office. Again, we see the role of unelected political staffers with limited accountability at the heart of modern governments. Just as the pre-parliamentary careers of politicians are more limited than they once were, so too are the pre-staffing backgrounds of political advisers. Where ministers are able to exert influence beyond their role in Cabinet, informal groupings such as Rudd's gang of four and Morrison's magnificent seven widen the rule of government a little beyond the PMO, but not nearly enough. And, of course, they undermine the formal Cabinet decision-making process.

Voters feel they are ruled and not governed by their politicians. Backbenchers feel similarly about the executive, and the executive is increasingly ruled by one office—that of the prime minister. The rise of the National Cabinet adds another layer of rule over the rest of us.

Another advantage of proportional representation—either introduced into the Lower House or once again respected in the Senate—is that it would necessitate consultation and bargaining between powerful actors in the political system. This bargaining is already a feature of the current system, but it is opaque: the Liberal–National coalition itself and the factions within parties make deals without regard for the public interest. Institutionalising bargaining will change public expectations of elections, and in turn move the political culture away from adversarialism. It lends itself to ongoing political engagement amongst the public, rather than conformity to a virtual 'elected dictatorship' model of heading to the polls once every three years.

There are aspects of Australian political culture that we take for granted, such as the theatre of budget night. Why should the contents of the government's Budget, it's most important document, be drip-fed to the media over weeks and even months, only for the treasurer to pull a rabbit out of a hat with a flourish? British governments release a budget Green Paper prepared by the Treasury with a number of taxation and expenditure options. This is a much more mature approach to policymaking, one worthy of further consideration.

One of the reasons for the failure of the two-party system is that society is simply too complex. Parties are tribal in a way that cuts across the issues-based interests of most voters. Recent history is littered with occasions where narrow consultation produced poorly thought-out policy that was reversed after a revolt led by a public or interest group. Governments tend to have a static or proforma view of consultation. Parliament has set up useful organs for investigating legislation and abuses of power, which are subject to the demands of the major political parties.

Another limitation is the contrast between the methods of mass-media control and the more egalitarian spirit of the internet. The role of social media in reducing politicians to actors in an ongoing political satire is a more recent phenomenon in this arms race. It has caused a lot of cynicism among older politicians in particular, such as Tony Abbott's dismissal of Twitter as 'electronic graffiti'. While we should be wary of which socioeconomic groups are dominating these new forms of interaction, that is no reason to avoid exploring ways for government bodies—not just parties and the parliament—to seek public input into their activities. Participatory democracy is a concept that the public generally responds well to. For all the angst surrounding the same-sex marriage plebiscite, alongside assumptions that postal ballot responses might be low, it was a resounding success.

Some of these measures can be institutionalised, but only citizens can change the political culture. We should demand a higher-quality standard of debate from media, interest groups, leaders and parties alike. Despite more ways to directly engage with politicians, those who represent us have never been more out of touch. Despite more opportunities for voters to access their politicians, if only fleetingly via social media, few want to, and fewer still pay attention to the political contest. When we do pay attention, we are voyeurs into the theatre of politics, rather than the policy debates that really matter.

A CHANGE IN STATUS

We have no expectation that the major political parties will be falling over each other to adopt these pariah policies. However, neither is any given election campaign a road map to policy development in the subsequent parliament, let alone a precursor to capturing the longer-term political trajectory. With a mixed record of policy development over the last two decades, Australia can learn from policy successes here and overseas. So too is it important to consider the reasons for failure, which can come from an overly complicated approach, as has been the case with climate change, or the temptation to use policy as a sledgehammer in domestic debate, as we have seen on the politics of the Budget. The political system won't suddenly change to embrace the policies outlined here. However, a more stable leadership outlook for the major parties could see the return of policymaking for the longer term. With pressure to raise revenue and to respond to the climate emergency, governments will be in the market for new policies, and the pariah status of these ideas could quickly change.

ACKNOWLEDGEMENTS

Wayne would like to thank Professor Carol Johnson for her many years of inspirational leadership in the study of Australian politics. Peter would like to thank the few politicians who are interested in policy for the conversations they have initiated over the years. Once again, we both have Louise Adler to thank for getting us involved in this writing project. Finally, a very big thanks to our copyeditor, Paul Smitz, for helping us to better express our thoughts on paper. All errors, of course, remain ours.

REFERENCES

A Universal Basic Income

Garnaut, Ross, *Reset: Restoring Australia after the Pandemic Recession*, La Trobe University Press, Carlton, Vic., 2021, pp. 163–78.

Picketty, Thomas, *Capital in the Twenty-First Century*, Harvard University Press, London, 2014.

Stiglitz, Joseph E, *The Price of Inequality: How Today's Divided Society Endangers Our Future*, W.W. Norton & Company, New York, 2013.

The World Bank, *Exploring Universal Basic Income: A Guide to Navigating Concepts, Evidence, and Practices*, 2020, https://www.worldbank.org/en/topic/socialprotection/publication/exploring-universal-basic-income-a-guide-to-navigating-concepts-evidence-and-practices (viewed March 2021).

Till Death Do Us Part

Cigdem-Bayram, Melek, Rachel Ong and Gavin Wood, 'A New Look at the Channels from Housing to Employment Decisions', AHURI report no. 275, Australian Housing and Urban Research Institute, Melbourne, March 2017, https://www.ahuri.edu.au/research/final-reports/275 (viewed March 2021).

Gilding, M, 'The Abolition of Death Duties in Australia: A Comparative Perspective', paper presented at 'Social Causes, Private Lives', the annual conference of the Australian Sociological Association, Sydney, 2010.

Henry, Ken, *Australia's Future Tax System: Final Report*, Australian Government, Canberra, August 2010.

Piketty, T, E Saez and G Zucman, 'Rethinking Capital and Wealth Taxation', Mimeo, Paris School of Economics, 2013.

Richardson, D, 'Surprise Me When I'm Dead: Revisiting the Case for Estate Duties', discussion paper, Australia Institute, Canberra, February 2016.

Truman, M, 'A Perfect Tax?', *Taxation*, 2 March 2006.

Taxing the Family Home

Errington, Wayne and Peter van Onselen, *John Winston Howard: The Biography*, Melbourne University Press, Melbourne, 2007.

Martin, Peter, 'Cheap Stamp Duty for First Home Buyers: Victoria's Package Looks Good', *The Age*, 5 March 2017, http://www.theage.com.au/victoria/cheap-stamp-duty-for-first-home-buyers-victorias-package-looks-good-20170305-gur4ky.html (viewed March 2021).

Pascoe, Michael, 'Taxing the Family Home Is Very Taxing Indeed', *The Sydney Morning Herald*, 7 April 2016, http://www.smh.com.au/business/the-economy/taxing-the-family-home-is-very-taxing-indeed-20160407-go0exy.html (viewed March 2021).

The Climate Emergency

Garnaut, Ross, *Super-Power: Australia's Low-carbon Opportunity*, La Trobe University Press, Carlton, Vic., 2019.

Pearse, Rebecca, *Pricing Carbon in Australia: Contestation, the State and Market Failure*, Routledge, Sydney, 2017.

It's Not as Easy as ABC

News and Media Research Centre, 'Digital News Report: Australia 2020', University of Canberra, 2020.

Ricketson, Matthew, Katherine Murphy and Patrick Mullins, 'The Media', in Mark Evans, Michelle Grattan and Brendan McCaffrie, *From Turnbull to Morrison— The Trust Divide: Australian Commonwealth Administration 2016–2019*, Melbourne University Press, Carlton, Vic., pp. 109–26, 2019.

The Sweetest Tax of All

World Health Organization, 'Taxes on Sugary Drinks: Why Do It?', 2017.

Where to from Here?

Mann, T, and N Ornstein (eds), *The Permanent Campaign and Its Future*, AEI Press, Washington, 2000.

van Onselen, Peter, *Professionals or Part-Timers? Major Party Senators in Australia*, Melbourne University Press, Melbourne, 2015.

van Onselen, Peter, and Wayne Errington, 'Ruling, Not Governing', in *Griffith Review 51: Fixing the System*, January 2016, pp. 105–16.

Ward, Ian, 'Mapping the Australian PR State', in S Young (ed.), *Government Communication in Australia*, Cambridge University Press, Melbourne, 2007.